November 2015

Pat,

Thank you for answering Tiffany Hill and becoming our guests. Hope the pages of my Dream Come True inspire you!

Helen

Breakfast at Tiffany Hill
Experience the Dream
Creative Team

Kate Moore   Susan Terrana

Donna Southwick   Selena Einwechter

Breakfast at Tiffany Hill

Experience the Dream

By Selena Einwechter
Food Photography by Jen Lepkowski

Written by: Selena Einwechter
Food Photography: Jen Lepkowski of Jen Lepkowski Photography
Editor: Susan Terrana

Susan Terrana   Jen Lepkowski
Selena Einwechter

Cover Design: Leslie Logemann of Logemann Design, Inc.
Contributing Personal Chefs: Donna Southwick of D'vine Kitchens
                                  Kate Moore of Bed & Breakfast on Tiffany Hill
Contributing Photographers: Cindy McDavid, John Einwechter, Claire Turner,
                                  and Steven Matthews

Library of Congress Cataloging-in-Publication Data:
ISBN 978-0-578-10731-8

Printed in the United States
By Signature Book Printing   www.sbpbooks.com

Table of Contents

Introduction
4 - 5

Thank You
8

Fruit Course
9 - 21

Sweet Breakfast
25 - 45

Savory Breakfast
49 - 77

Dessert Course
80 - 93

Follow Your Dream
94 - 96

Introduction

Welcome to Breakfast at Tiffany Hill! For several years now, I've been greeting old friends and new as they've gathered in the mornings around the grand dining room table at the Bed & Breakfast on Tiffany Hill.

My 25-year dream come true, this custom-built inn is cradled in the cozy pastoral community of Mills River, North Carolina. Here the atmosphere of casual elegance filled with Southern hospitality seeps into guests' souls, beckoning them to return time and time again. Boasting seven stunning suites on a six-acre property, the bed & breakfast quickly earned bragging rights with its Select Registry distinction and praise from national press.

I've been blessed beyond belief to see such success in three short years. But when it comes to day-to-day innkeeping, my pleasure is found in delighting my guests and my God. Hence the labor of love you're holding in your hands. You see, after years of hearing happy diners ask for recipes, I couldn't help but satisfy their senses with this beautiful book. What a joy it is to offer this collection of my favorite Southern recipes – gathered from friends, family and magazines – so that guests may take home a piece of their experience at Tiffany Hill!

This is very much a first for me. It's not uncommon for guests to ask to be in the kitchen while I cook – but I've always sent them away toward the end, claiming it was "time to make the magic happen." I never gave away all my secrets until this cookbook. But I also see beauty in inspiration, and I can't wait to show you how easy it is to whip up a gourmet breakfast in your own home.

Of course to host an authentic breakfast like those served here at Tiffany Hill, two treasured traditions must be honored. First, you must celebrate something. Whether silly or heart-felt, being thankful every morning when we rise puts a positive spin on the day. So choose what you're celebrating – good health, lovely weather, lasting love, or timeless friendship – and take a moment to savor it.

The second tradition is even sweeter. Yes, dear ones, eat dessert first. I'm giving you permission! Don't let dinnertime have all the fun - make breakfast memorable by ending it on a sweet note. We have but one life, and it's worth delighting in every last dollop of parfait, strawberry crepe or chocolate molten cake.

All that said, although breakfast is something to celebrate, preparing it should never leave the hostess ragged. Here in my kitchen, I go by the saying, "if it isn't easy, I'm not cooking it." You can't serve a three-course breakfast every morning unless the process is painless. Not only are these recipes easy, they're also perfected. Each of these 49 recipes has a tried-and-true Tiffany Hill stamp of approval. We know this by the clean plates coming back from our guests!

Let the stunning images on these pages inspire your presentation. Much of the joy of hosting is adding beauty to your table. Again, this doesn't mean you'll spend extra time slaving away. Allow Mother Nature to do the heavy lifting. One of the most beautiful plates in this book is the rainbow of fruit on page 12 - no cooking was required, yet the presentation packs a punch.

From there, complement your culinary spread with a beautiful table. What a wonderful excuse to break out the fine china, clip fresh flowers, and iron lovely linens. I've been using my china every day, long before opening the bed & breakfast. Use it; enjoy it! Let our place setting shots offer a launching point for your table.

As you flip through these pages, you'll see we've dreamed up more than a simple set of recipes. Rather, *Breakfast at Tiffany Hill* offers a keepsake memento of the inn featuring stunning photography of the suites and the gardens, as well as an inspirational account of my journey to fulfilling my life's dream. My purpose with this project was very intentional: I want you, my sweet friends, to know that you too can achieve anything you put your mind to - beginning with breakfast.

It is my deepest desire that you'll find endless ideas and inspiration from *Breakfast at Tiffany Hill.* I can't wait to hear tales and testimonies of many magical moments around your own table. Enjoy!

Selena

Bed & Breakfast on Tiffany Hill

A Place for All Seasons

Thank You!

"Thank-yous" come easy for me! I've had a lot of practice with all who have supported my dream for so many years. But when you have just one page and less than 600 words, it's tough!

Like any good Southern woman, I've collected recipes for decades, pored over them, tested them on friends and tweaked them to make them my own! Donna Southwick has worked with me over the years to hone my breakfast offerings. Her skills as a Southern cook, kitchen organizer and food expert have come to life through D'vine Kitchen, an Atlanta based company offering in home services to help busy people put healthy food on their tables. So proud of you my friend for following your passion! I thank you for all of your culinary expertise.

I love being an innkeeper! But, after 2 ½ years of doing it alone, I was blessed when Kate Moore joined me in the kitchen. As Tiffany Hill's breakfast chef, Kate has added her flair to our breakfast menus. Behind the scenes, but yet a huge part of Tiffany Hill is Sabine Mata, head of operations. Without her, we could not have focused on this project. Thank you both for bringing more joy to Tiffany Hill.

You will be dazzled by Jen Lepkowski's food photography. That photo shoot weekend will be embossed in the memories of all who participated. What an amazing time! Leslie of Logemann Design made us look good with her creative cover design. Writer extraordinaire, Lauren Eberle, assisted putting thoughts to paper to communicate what is in my heart. Thank you ladies for your patience and persistence in bringing this part of the dream to reality!

A few other participants; Tracy Benden, Laura Crawley, Kristen Finkelstein, and Pam Schnurr, all lent their best china so that we could showcase each dish. Melinda DeRouin, Michele Huggett, and Tracy Cavagnaro all spent endless hours poring over each page to make sure we dotted every "i" and crossed every "t"! Thank you all!

A world of gratitude goes to my editor Susan Terrana! You would not be holding this book had it not been for a certain breakfast at Tiffany's where a seed was planted. A dream, goal, or project begins with a first seed. It does not hurt to do research or take a first step. The biggest mistake is when you do not try. God knits us together in His way for His good. Susan and I have been knitted together through Tiffany Hill. We both reached for the stars and succeeded. Susan, you came as a guest, left as a friend, became my editor and we are now knit together forever through *Breakfast at Tiffany Hill; Experience the Dream.*

There is a world of people not mentioned here who have encouraged me over the decades to pursue my dream. The result is this collection of beautiful pictures of Tiffany Hill and the story of a dream fulfilled. But it has been Tiffany Hill's guests, with their continual requests for recipes as well as a commemorative of the B&B, who have inspired me to do this book. I am so thankful for their encouragement, support, and the new friendships made with each visit. I love my Dream Come True! Thanks to all of you!

Fruit Course

Ambrosia

Breakfast Bananas Foster

Fruit Plate

Fruit and Yogurt Parfait

Ginger Fruit by D'vine Kitchen

Layered Fruit Salad

Local Apple Sauté with Homemade Granola

Homemade Granola

Melon with Honey Cream

Strawberries 'N Cream

Summer Peach Soup

Vanilla Citrus Salad

Ambrosia

This classic Southern fruit dish is best served with a savory breakfast. We like to include pecans in our Southern classic. Enjoy!

1 can (20 oz.) pineapple chunks, drained	1½ cups seedless grapes
1 can (11 or 15 oz.) mandarin oranges, drained	½ cup miniature marshmallows
1 banana, sliced	½ cup pecans, chopped
	1 cup vanilla low-fat yogurt
	¼ cup flaked coconut, toasted

Combine pineapple chunks, mandarin oranges, banana, grapes, marshmallows and pecans in a medium bowl. Stir yogurt into fruit mixture. Sprinkle with coconut.

Serves 10

On Tiffany Hill, we celebrate something every day.

Innkeeper Tidbit:
You might be tempted to leave the marshmallows out, but don't. There's a little kid in all of us!

Breakfast Bananas Foster

This recipe was a solution to all the bananas that were going to waste at the B&B. Guests do not eat fresh fruit as much as you would think. Although we love to have it available for those who enjoy it, we hate to toss it. So this recipe was created to use up those bananas. Guests have thoroughly enjoyed our solution!

½ **cup butter**
1 **cup brown sugar**
1 **cup whipping cream**

1 **cup pecans, chopped**
5 **bananas, sliced**

In a sauce pan, melt the butter and brown sugar. Over medium heat, gradually stir in cream, and then stir in the pecans. Slice bananas into individual, small fruit bowls. Spoon a small amount of sauce over the bananas.

Serves 10

We serve a three course gourmet breakfast daily. Everything from fruit to dessert!

Innkeeper Tidbit:
You can make a large batch of the Foster and refrigerate what you don't use for the next time.

Fruit Plate

Use a variety of colors to make this dish eye appealing. There is nothing better than a wonderful collection of fruits to start your day. Simple and elegant, and so easy to do!

2 apples, cored and sliced
2 oranges, sliced
10 bunches of grapes
3 kiwis, peeled and sliced
30 dried apricots

Arrange on medium plates using a complement of colors.

Serves 10

One guest referred to our fruit course as a "fruit appetizer".

Innkeeper Tidbit:
We try to have a variety of five fruits on each plate.

Fruit & Yogurt Parfait

Vanilla yogurt, paired with fresh strawberries and bananas, topped with our Homemade Granola makes this a simple and classic fruit dish to serve with a sweet breakfast.

3 bananas, sliced
32 oz. vanilla yogurt
5 strawberries, sliced
½ cup Homemade Granola (page 17)

Divide sliced bananas in bottom of 10 parfait glasses. Add yogurt, followed by strawberries. Top with a dollop more yogurt and Homemade Granola.

Serves 10

*On Tiffany Hill, come as guests,
leave as friends.*

Innkeeper Tidbit:
Out of strawberries? No problem. Use blueberries or peaches, instead!

Ginger Fruit by D'vine Kitchen

Donna came up with the idea to pull together various fruits of the same color to create this beautiful eye opener. Topped with a ginger ale sauce, this dish sparkles!

3 cups honeydew chunks
3 kiwi fruit
1 ½ cups seedless green
grapes, halved
¾ cup ginger ale

3 Tbsp. shredded coconut + 2 Tbsp.
1 Tbsp. ginger spice paste
2 tsp. pistachios

Cut skin off kiwi and cut kiwi and honeydew into bite size pieces. Wash grapes and cut in half. Place all fruit in a salad bowl. Whisk ginger ale, 3 Tbsp. coconut, and ginger paste until blended. Pour mixture over fruit; let stand 5 to 10 minutes for flavors to blend. Stir and serve in martini glasses or small bowls. Sprinkle with remaining coconut, and pistachios.

Serves 10

*Come and do as much or
as little as you like
on Tiffany Hill.*

Innkeeper Tidbit:
Instead of using the ginger spice paste, try substituting fresh grated ginger for an even fresher, brighter ginger flavor.

Layered Fruit Salad

Have fun with this one! Find a small trifle dish so that the stacking of colors showcases the fruit. The success of this dish is the Honey Orange Sauce. So simple and so delicious!

10 grapes, halved
¼ apple, cut into pieces
8 slices mandarin oranges
10 slices of banana
5 pieces of kiwi

Honey Orange Sauce
¼ cup orange juice
¼ cup honey

For the sauce, stir orange juice and honey together so that it is well blended.

Arrange fruit in layers, starting with the grapes and ending with kiwi on top. Pour enough Honey Orange Sauce over fruit to cover the grapes on the bottom (or more if you like).

Serves 1

Rise and shine,
it's
breakfast time!

Innkeeper Tidbit:
Don't be surprised when your guests pick up the dish and drink the sauce. It's really that good!

Local Apple Sauté with Homemade Granola

Thank you Rachel Reid, for showing me this delicious fruit dish! I loved our times in the kitchen together. What makes this dish special is the fabulous granola.

1 apple, thinly sliced
2 Tbsp. sugar
2 Tbsp. butter
Cinnamon

Vanilla yogurt
Homemade Granola (page 17)

Toss the apple slices with sugar. Over medium heat, melt the butter in a sauté pan. Add apples. Sprinkle with cinnamon to taste. Allow apples to sauté until tender. You can then turn off stove and let them sit until ready to serve. Top with a dollop of vanilla yogurt and our Homemade Granola.

Serves 2

Holly Golightly liked having Breakfast at Tiffany's because nothing bad ever happened there.

Innkeeper Tidbit:
We use vintage Golden Delicious apples from Holt Orchards in Hendersonville.

Homemade Granola

Make this ahead to have on hand. Use it for a topping on fruit, ice cream, or even as a main dish with milk. Oh, so good!

6 cups old fashioned rolled oats
2 cups sliced almonds
1 cup raw pumpkin seeds
1 cup sunflower seeds
1 cup brown sugar, firmly packed

½ cup honey, heated
1/3 cup canola oil
1 tsp. vanilla extract
1/8 tsp. salt
1 cup dried cranberries

Preheat oven to 350°.

With cooking spray, seriously grease 2 heavy duty 12 by 17 cookie sheets with a lip. In a large bowl, stir together the first 5 ingredients. Heat the honey and combine with the oil, vanilla and salt. Pour over dry ingredients and mix well. Divide and spread the granola mixture onto greased cookie sheets. Bake for 20 minutes and stir. Pay attention as it will brown quickly! Cook for another 10 to 15 minutes or until golden brown. Remove from oven and thoroughly mix in cranberries. Cool, then break into smaller pieces and store in an air tight container.

Frugal is fun!

Innkeeper Tidbit:
A batch of this Homemade Granola makes a great housewarming gift or unique gifts for your friends during the holidays!

Melon with Honey Cream

A little bit goes a long way with this dish. It is all about the presentation. Serving melon can sometimes be challenging. By layering a plate with "flights" of melon medallions drizzled with our Honey Cream Sauce ... well, the plates come back clean every time!

½ **cantaloupe, sliced**
½ **honeydew, sliced**
Fresh berries, for garnish

Honey Cream Sauce
4 tsp. vanilla yogurt
2 tsp. honey

Have fun arranging pieces of melon on dish.

For the sauce, mix yogurt and honey together. Drizzle over fruit and serve. Garnish with fresh berries, if desired.

Serves 10

Enjoy the journey!

Innkeeper Tidbit:
We use melon that is in season. We incorporate watermelon during the summer for variation. We love using locally produced Sourwood honey!

Strawberries 'N Cream

While I worked in England for a year, I enjoyed having this dish often. Simple and delicious, the secret is definitely in the sauce!

1 pint strawberries
1 cup heavy whipping cream
Hazelnut liqueur

Cut strawberries into pieces and divide between serving bowls. Mix whipping cream with liqueur, to taste, making sure they are well blended. Pour over fruit.

Serves 10

"Guests bloom in their rooms."
~ Cassandra Clark

Innkeeper Tidbit:
Play around with the cream additives to come up with your own favorite. Almost anything will work and it is easy to do!

Summer Peach Soup

Inspired by a magazine picture of fruit, this pinwheel concept of peaches and blueberries has been enjoyed by many a guest!

5 fresh peaches, sliced
Fresh blueberries
½ cup Mint Simple Syrup

<u>**Mint Simple Syrup**</u>
1 cup water
1 cup sugar
6 sprigs of mint

For the syrup, bring water to a boil. Stir in sugar until it dissolves. Add cleaned mint leaves into pot. Turn heat off and let sit for 30 minutes. Pour into a container and refrigerate overnight.

In the morning, arrange peach slices in a pinwheel design with blueberries in between. Pour chilled Mint Syrup over the fruit and serve.

Serves 10

Every day is a blessing.

Innkeeper Tidbit:
Use fresh mint from your garden for the Mint Simple Syrup. We enjoy using different varieties from spearmint to pineapple mint.

Vanilla Citrus Salad

Sometimes fruit just needs a little something to make it special. Using simple syrup with the tartness of the grapefruit makes this a winner!

2 cans mandarin oranges
2 cups grapefruit, deveined
½ cup Vanilla Simple Syrup

<u>**Vanilla Simple Syrup**</u>
1 cup water
1 cup sugar
1 vanilla bean

For the syrup, bring water to a boil. Stir in sugar until it dissolves. Break vanilla bean into 3 pieces and drop into pot. Turn heat off and let sit for 30 minutes. Pour into a container and refrigerate overnight.

In the morning, mix fruit and Vanilla Simple Syrup together. Chill for 1 hour before serving.

Serves 8

Celebrate new discoveries every day!

Innkeeper Tidbit:
Vanilla beans can be expensive, but are worth it to make this recipe work. Use ½ cup of syrup for the recipe and save the other ½ for next time. It keeps in the refrigerator for a long time.

The Main House Suites

Seaside Suite

Beaufort Suite

Madison Suite

Natchez Suite

Lexington Suite

The Carriage House Suites

Mountain Brook Suite

Sweet Breakfast Course

Apple Country French Toast

Banana Pineapple Bread French Toast

Key Lime French Toast

Loaded Berry Waffle

Peaches & Cream French Toast

Pecan Praline French Toast

Pineapple Upside Down French Toast

Strawberry Challah Breakfast Pudding

Stuffed French Toast

Sweet Potato Pancakes

Apple Country French Toast

Tiffany Hill is located in Henderson County, North Carolina's #1 apple producing area! Harvest season begins mid-August and apples are available through December. *Our absolute favorite apples are the vintage varieties that come from Holt Orchards!* We enjoy the apple season with this special French toast.

1 loaf French bread
5 large eggs
1½ cups milk
1 tsp. vanilla extract
1 cup light brown sugar, firmly packed

½ cup butter or margarine
2 Tbsp. light corn syrup
8 Golden Delicious apples,
 peeled and sliced
Whipped cream
Cinnamon

Cut bread into ¾-inch thick slices. Place in a single layer in a lightly greased 9 by 13-inch baking dish. Wisk eggs, milk, and vanilla together and pour over bread. Cover and chill for 8 hours, or overnight.

In the morning, preheat oven to 350°.

Remove bread from dish. Wipe dish clean; coat with cooking spray. Cook brown sugar, butter and syrup in a saucepan, over low heat, stirring often until mixture is smooth. Pour into baking dish. Top with apples; arrange bread over apples.

Bake for 40 minutes. Loosen with knife; invert onto platter. Top with whipped cream and sprinkle with cinnamon.

Serves 10

Innkeeper Tidbit:
A morning time saving tip: Slice the apples the night before and use Fruit-Fresh so they do not turn brown. Then you are ready to go in the morning!

Banana Pineapple Bread French Toast

Adapted from my sister's favorite banana bread recipe, we have added pineapple to make this a Tiffany Hill favorite.

1/3 **cup shortening**
1/3 **cup sugar**
2 eggs + 1 egg
1¾ **cups flour, sifted**
½ **tsp. baking soda**
½ **tsp. salt**

1 tsp. baking powder
¾ **cup ripe bananas, mashed**
¾ **cup crushed pineapple**
2 tsp. banana extract
1 cup milk

Preheat oven to 350°.

Cream together shortening and sugar, add 2 eggs and beat well. Sift together dry ingredients. Add bananas and pineapple alternately to creamed mixture, blending well after each addition. Stir in extract.

Pour into well-greased 9 by 5 by 3-inch loaf pan. Bake for 45 to 50 minutes or until center is set and bread is golden brown. Remove from pan. Cool on rack.

Mix the remaining egg with milk. Slice Banana Pineapple Bread into 1-inch thick slices. Dip each bread slice in egg mixture and place on griddle until golden brown, turning once.

Top with warm pineapple and maple syrup.

Serves 8

Innkeeper Tidbit:
Our breakfast chef, Kate Moore, was inspired by a Jamaican favorite on her honeymoon. We took a Southern staple of banana bread and made it a delicious morning French toast! Experimenting with recipes can result in new favorites.

Key Lime French Toast

This favorite summer recipe was given to us by guests, Sarah and Ken Schwartz, who had enjoyed it at Graystone Inn in Wilmington, NC. After testing it on a group of friends, it received a "thumbs up" and joined our collection of guest favorites!

Batter
2 large loaves day-old French bread
7 large eggs
1 cup milk
3 Tbsp. sugar
1 tsp. vanilla extract
2 Tbsp. butter (for cooking)

Lime Cream Filling
16 oz. cream cheese
3 Tbsp. lime juice
7 Tbsp. sugar
Zest of 5 limes

Preheat oven to 350°.

For the filling, in a small bowl, mix together all ingredients, blending well.

Slice off each end of the bread and discard. Cut next slice ½-inch thick and only three quarters of the way through the loaf to form a pocket. Cut the next ½-inch slice all the way through. Continue to do this until all of the bread is sliced. Spread 1 Tbsp. of filling in each pocket and press together.

For the batter, in a large bowl, whisk together eggs, milk, sugar and vanilla.

Preheat a large, nonstick griddle to 350°. Add 1 Tbsp. butter to coat the griddle. Dip each slice of stuffed bread in batter, turning to coat. When the butter on the griddle foams, add bread slices and cook until lightly browned; about 3 minutes on each side, turning once. Remove from griddle and place on a sheet pan. Add remaining butter to skillet and repeat. Place sheet pan in preheated oven 15 minutes before serving the French toast.

Serves 10

Innkeeper Tidbit:
If fresh limes are not available, you can substitute Nellie and Joe's Key West Lime Juice.

Loaded Berry Waffle

I love this dish presentation! Of course, you may not have the Belgian waffle irons, so use what you have. We were very fortunate that our friend, Michele Huggett, was persistent in finding these for Tiffany Hill.

¾ **cup granulated sugar**
½ **cup (1 stick) unsalted butter, softened**
2 **large eggs**
2 **tsp. vanilla extract**
1½ **cups all-purpose flour**

½ **tsp. salt**
¼ **tsp. baking powder**
¼ **tsp. baking soda**
½ **cup buttermilk**
3 **cups fresh mixed berries**

Preheat waffle iron.

In mixing bowl, beat sugar and butter until light and fluffy, stopping to scrape bowl occasionally. Beat in eggs, one at a time, until blended. Add vanilla. In a small bowl, whisk together flour, salt, baking powder and baking soda to blend well. On low speed, add flour mixture in 3 parts, alternately with buttermilk, in 2 parts. Mix just until blended, stopping to scrape bowl often. Batter will be very thick. Let rest at room temperature before baking.

In a saucepan, bring fresh berries to a simmer, adding a splash of water if needed.

Spoon batter onto the hot, greased waffle iron and bake. Top with warm berries.

Serves 6 to 8

Innkeeper Tidbit:
Add maple syrup to your berries as they simmer to give them a touch of sweetness!

Peaches & Cream French Toast

There's nothing like peaches and cream together! This French toast celebrates this pairing. You can use either croissants or French bread to make this luscious dish.

1 cup brown sugar
½ cup sweet cream butter
2 Tbsp. corn syrup
1 bag frozen, sliced peaches
5-6 croissants (large light type)
   or 1 loaf sliced French bread
1 (8 oz.) package cream cheese
1 dozen eggs
1½ cups half & half
1 tsp. vanilla extract

Grease a 9 by 13-inch, or larger, baking dish. Melt brown sugar, butter, and corn syrup in a sauce pan until bubbly. Pour mixture into the baking dish. Spread peaches over the caramel syrup. Break the bread into pieces and place over the peaches. Cut cream cheese into little pieces and scatter throughout the breaks (in little pillow-like puffs).

In a blender, mix the eggs, half & half and vanilla. Pour over the bread, cover, and refrigerate overnight.

In the morning, place into a cold oven and bake at 350° for 45 minutes. You can cover the top if it is getting too brown. When it is nearly finished, it will begin to puff up and you will see the caramel bubbling up.

Serves 8

Innkeeper Tidbit:
Fresh peaches are good, but frozen peaches are easier and more consistent.

Pecan Praline French Toast

When you live in the South, you *must* use pecans in your cooking! This is a delicious way to celebrate the South!

 ½ **cup light brown sugar, firmly packed**
 ½ **cup butter or margarine**
 2 Tbsp. light corn syrup
 ¾ **cup pecans, chopped**
 1 loaf French bread, sliced into 6 (2-inch) pieces
 6 large eggs
 ½ **cup half & half**
 1 tsp. maple syrup

Stir together first 4 ingredients in a small saucepan. Cook over low heat, stirring often, until butter melts and mixture is smooth. Pour into a lightly greased 9 by 13-inch baking dish. Place French bread in a single layer over syrup. Whisk together eggs and last 2 ingredients; pour over bread. Cover and chill for 8 hours, or overnight.

In the morning, preheat oven to 350°.

Remove from refrigerator and let stand at room temperature for 30 minutes. Bake for 45 minutes. Serve immediately.

Serves 6

Innkeeper Tidbit:
You can make this in a big dish. Just be sure not to crowd the pieces of bread so that they keep their shape when serving.

Pineapple Upside Down French Toast

What is a stay at Tiffany Hill without our signature French toast? Well, it just wouldn't be complete! This is our favorite, and so easy to make that you will surely be enjoying breakfast from Tiffany Hill in your own home with your guests! Please think of us when you do!

2 Tbsp. butter
¼ cup brown sugar
½ cup crushed pineapple, drained well
1 egg, beaten
1½ cups milk
8 slices thick-cut raisin cinnamon bread

8 maraschino cherries
Powdered sugar

Preheat oven to 350°.

Melt butter and pour into the bottom of a 9 by 13-inch glass baking dish. Sprinkle brown sugar on butter and blend well. Layer the pineapple into the mixture.

In a bowl, mix milk with beaten egg. Dip bread slices into milk and egg mixture. Place bread over pineapple. Bake for 30 minutes or until golden brown.

Invert onto plate and top with maraschino cherry and powdered sugar.

Serves 8

Innkeeper Tidbit:
The secret to this recipe is the bread! Our favorite comes from Atlanta Bread Company.

Strawberry Challah Breakfast Pudding

Guests lobbied me to change the name of this French toast to pudding as it is so creamy. A version of this was featured in the November/December 2011 SavorNC Magazine.

1 loaf Challah bread, cubed
8 oz. strawberry cream cheese
6 large eggs
4 cups half & half
½ cup butter, melted
¼ cup maple syrup

Strawberry Sauce
1 pint fresh strawberries
1 (8 oz.) jar strawberry preserves

Place ½ of cubed bread in a 9 by 13-inch pan which has been sprayed with cooking spray. Sprinkle with ½ teaspoons of cream cheese, using all 8 ounces. Arrange remaining bread on top. Whisk together eggs, half & half, melted butter and maple syrup. Pour over bread and cream cheese, pressing down to absorb egg mixture. Cover and chill in refrigerator for 8 hours, or overnight.

In the morning, preheat oven to 350°. Bake covered for 30 minutes. Uncover and continue baking for 20 minutes. Allow to rest for 5 minutes before cutting.

For the sauce, slice strawberries and place in saucepan. Add preserves and simmer for 15 minutes. Ladle strawberry sauce over toast. Sauce can be chilled overnight, but warm it before serving.

Serves 8

Innkeeper Tidbit:
Our Christmas Challah Pudding is shown here. We use cranberries and simple syrup to dress it up during the holiday season.

Stuffed French Toast

Adapted from a recipe graciously provided by Linda Hayes, my B&B mentor, this recipe is a guest favorite. Thank you Linda!

Filling
6 oz. cream cheese, softened
½ cup honey
½ cup finely chopped nuts

12 pieces white bread
Butter
Powdered sugar

Batter
1½ cups milk
5 large eggs
1/3 cup all-purpose flour
2 Tbsp. sugar
2/3 Tbsp. baking powder
2/3 Tbsp. vanilla
1/3 tsp. salt

Preheat oven to 350°.

For the filling, mix together all ingredients.

In a separate bowl, mix all batter ingredients.

Spread filling on bread. Top with second piece of bread. In a skillet, melt butter over medium heat. Dip each stuffed "sandwich" into batter and cook on hot skillet until golden brown, turning over when ready. Transfer to a baking sheet, and place in the preheated oven to continue cooking. Bake the slices until puffed and golden, about 9 minutes. Remove from oven and sprinkle with powdered sugar.

Serves 6

Innkeeper Tidbit:
Try switching the recipe up with an optional filling of 6 oz. cream cheese, softened and mixed with ½ cup fruit preserves (blackberry, peach, strawberry or orange marmalade).

Sweet Potato Pancakes

Now I'm really giving our secrets away! This recipe is so simple and guests love the fluffy twist on traditional pancakes!

Pancake Batter
½ cup Bruce's Sweet Potato
    Pancake Mix
½ cup Krusteaz Buttermilk
    Pancake Mix
¾ cup water
1 tsp. vanilla extract

Butter
Maple syrup

Mix all ingredients together and let rest for 15 minutes. Preheat griddle. Ladle ¼ cup pancake mix on to griddle for each pancake, turning once.

Serve with butter and hot maple syrup.

Serves 4

Innkeeper Tidbit:
I never thought we would make pancakes on Tiffany Hill, but this recipe is so good and so easy, we couldn't resist! Thanks Rachel!

The Gardens of Tiffany Hill

True
Owner
~
Tuxedo

Savory Breakfast Course

Artichoke Ham Strata

Baked Herb Eggs

Basil Boursin Potato Tart with Chive Eggs by D'vine Kitchen

Breakfast Empanada by D'vine Kitchen

Breakfast Trifle

Brie Sausage Strata

Cass' Egg Mushroom Ham Cup

French Sorrel Quiche

Greek Frittata

Hash Brown Casserole with Chive Eggs

Lemon Basil Soufflé

Sunrise Pot Pie by D'vine Kitchen

Three Cheese Egg Croissants

Ultimate Cheese Omelet with Southern Grits

Artichoke Ham Strata

This is a no-fail, go-to breakfast strata. It's great when hosting a brunch or having holiday guests stay overnight, since you just stick it in the oven in the morning. It's light, yet has lots of flavor. Everyone will ask for seconds!

3 English Muffins, split and cut into 1-inch squares	**1 (14 oz.) can artichoke hearts, drained and chopped**
2 Tbsp. butter, melted	**3 garlic cloves, minced**
1 cup lean ham, chopped	**1/8 tsp. ground nutmeg**
½ cup (2 oz.) fresh Parmesan cheese, grated	**1 (12 oz.) can evaporated milk**
2 Tbsp. fresh chives, chopped	**4 large eggs**
	4 egg whites

Spray 10 ramekins with cooking spray. Arrange muffin pieces in bottom of ramekins. Drizzle with melted butter. Layer the ham and the next 4 ingredients over muffin pieces. Mix remaining ingredients and pour into ramekins. Cover and let sit overnight in the refrigerator.

In the morning, preheat oven to 375°. Bake for 25 minutes or until puffy and golden brown. Garnish with fresh chives.

Serves 10

Innkeeper Tidbit:
If you are serving vegetarian, simply omit the ham. A great accompaniment to this dish is rosemary potatoes.

Baked Herb Eggs

Thanks to my long-time friend, Clare Dixon, we have an herb garden on Tiffany Hill. When I was looking for ways to use my herbs in new breakfast dishes, I came up with this dish.

3 tomatoes, chopped
½ cup fresh basil, chopped (reserving some for garnish)
¼ cup fresh flat-leaf parsley, chopped (reserving some for garnish)
1 tsp. salt
1 tsp. freshly ground pepper

4 tsp. unsalted butter
8 eggs
8 tsp. heavy cream
8 tsp. grated Parmigiano-Reggiano cheese (optional)

Preheat oven to 350°. Generously butter 8 ramekins.

In a bowl, stir together tomatoes, basil, parsley, ½ tsp. of the salt, and ½ tsp. of the pepper. Divide tomato mixture evenly among the prepared ramekins. Cut the 4 tsp. butter into small pieces and divide among the ramekins, sprinkling the pieces evenly over the tomato mixture. Break an egg into each ramekin. Season the egg with the remaining salt and pepper, dividing evenly. Drizzle 1 tsp. of the cream on each egg. Arrange the ramekins on a rimmed baking sheet.

Bake until the egg whites are opaque and the yolks have firm edges and are soft in the center, about 20 to 25 minutes. Remove from the oven and sprinkle each serving with 1 tsp. of the cheese and remaining herbs. Let stand a couple of minutes before serving.

Serves 8

Innkeeper Tidbit:
A variation is to add diced cooked red potatoes with the tomatoes for a heartier breakfast.

Basil Boursin Potato Tart by D'vine Kitchen

Who doesn't love Boursin cheese? Using this cheese, coupled with the basil, sets this potato dish above the rest!

½ round of Boursin cheese
1 cup heavy cream
4 Tbsp. fresh basil, minced
Salt and pepper

2 medium Idaho potatoes, peeled
** and thinly sliced**
1 tsp. Parmigiano-Reggiano cheese,
** freshly grated (to sprinkle on top)**
1 Tbsp. shredded Mozzarella cheese
** (to sprinkle on top)**

Preheat oven to 350°.

Coat 8 individual ramekins with olive oil.

Wisk Boursin cheese, heavy cream, and spices in a large bowl, adding salt and pepper to taste. Fold in the potatoes. Place mixture in individual ramekins and cover with shredded cheeses. Bake for 25 to 30 minutes. Serve along with Chive Eggs (page 68).

Serves 8

Innkeeper Tidbit:
We often serve cheese and crackers in the afternoon. I will never forget one guest's reaction when she tasted Boursin cheese for the first time. "It tastes just like butter! Paula would be pleased," she said.

Breakfast Empanada by D'vine Kitchen

A wonderfully hearty breakfast concept created by D'vine Kitchen. In the South, we love our white gravy and this empanada pairs very well with gravy!

3 refrigerated pie pastry sheets
1 cup cooked ham, diced
3 scrambled eggs (see Innkeeper Tidbit)
Salt and pepper
3/4 cup grated Cheddar cheese
Egg wash (1 beaten egg with 1 Tbsp. water)

Preheat oven to 375°.

Cut 6 (6-inch) rounds of pie pastry. Place 2 Tbsp. diced ham on each pastry round, top with 1/6 of scrambled eggs, and salt and pepper to taste. Sprinkle with 2 Tbsp. of cheese. Fold pastry over in half, seal edges with small amount of water on your fingertips, and crimp edges like a pie crust. Place on a cookie sheet, brush with egg wash, and bake for 20 minutes or until golden brown.

Serves 6

Innkeeper Tidbit:
When preparing scrambled eggs for this recipe, cook the eggs till set, but not dry. Eggs will continue to cook inside the empanada. They will be perfect when the empanada comes out of the oven!

Breakfast Trifle

Donna from D'vine Kitchen comes to Tiffany Hill frequently for recipe development. The Breakfast Trifle is a result of one of our weekend cook-a-thons.

2 cups water	8 breakfast sausage patties
1 cup half & half	1 cup Cheddar cheese, shredded
1 cup stone ground grits	1 tomato, chopped
3 Tbsp. butter	Sour cream, (optional)
Salt	Chopped chives (optional)
8 eggs, hard boiled	

Southern Grits:
Bring water and half & half to a boil. Slowly add in grits while stirring. Reduce heat. Add butter and salt and simmer until cooked, stirring occasionally.

Hard Boiled Eggs:
Add eggs to a medium saucepan and cover with cold water. Bring to a rapid boil then turn off heat and let the eggs sit for 20 minutes. Let cool, then peel and rough chop.

Sausage Patties:
Place sausage patties in a preheated skillet over medium heat. Cook 4 to 5 minutes per side, until done. Chop coarsely.

Assemble Mini Breakfast Trifles:
Spoon grits equally into 10 trifle bowls. Sprinkle with shredded cheese. Add chopped hard boiled eggs. Spoon chopped sausage on top of the eggs. Add the tomato on top of the sausage. Garnish with a dollop of sour cream and chopped chives.

Serves 10

Innkeeper Tidbit:
We only use stone ground grits from Nora Mill in North Georgia for our recipes.

Brie Sausage Strata

On Tiffany Hill, we like to serve 3 course, plated breakfasts. This recipe was adapted from a Southern Living Magazine recipe. The difference is the individual portions. You can break any casserole into individual ramekins, then, simply reduce the cooking time in half.

3 white bread crusts, cubed
1 cup cooked pork sausage
4 oz. Brie cheese
½ cup grated Parmesan cheese

3 large eggs
1½ cups whipped cream
1 cup fat-free milk
½ tsp. seasoned salt
½ tsp. dry mustard

Spray 6 ramekins with cooking spray. Place bread crusts in bottom. Layer sausage, then bits of Brie (just rip it apart). Next, cover with Parmesan cheese. Mix remaining ingredients together and divide evenly into each ramekin.

Cover and refrigerate overnight.

In the morning, preheat oven to 350°. Bake for 25 minutes or until puffy and golden brown.

Garnish with chopped green onions or any herb you have on hand.

Serves 6

Innkeeper Tidbit:
We like to serve this dish with sweet potato medallions which are very easy to make. Scrub potato well. Cut in 1-inch rounds. Toss with olive oil and salt and bake for 45 minutes, turning once. We always have cooked ground sausage in the freezer. Defrost in the microwave and you are ready to go, without having to cook sausage in the morning!

Cass' Egg Mushroom Ham Cup

Cassandra Clark was my first B&B mentor. I was thrilled when she accepted my offer that I hoped she wouldn't refuse. If she would teach me everything about her B&B, I would gladly work for free. Thank you Cassandra for showing me that I could do it! Here is one of her favorite recipes.

¾ lb. mushrooms, finely chopped	2 Tbsp. crème fraise or sour cream
¼ cup shallot, finely chopped	1 Tbsp. fresh tarragon, finely chopped
2 Tbsp. unsalted butter	12 slices Black Forest or Virginia
½ tsp. salt	ham (without holes; 10 oz.)
¼ tsp. black pepper	12 large eggs

Preheat oven to 400°.

Prepare Mushrooms:
Cook mushrooms and shallots in butter, with salt and pepper, in a large heavy skillet over moderately high heat. Stir until mushrooms are tender and liquid is evaporated, about 10 minutes. Remove from heat and stir in sour cream and tarragon.

Assemble and bake:
Place 1 slice of ham into each of 12 lightly oiled muffin cups (ends will stick up and hang over edges of cups). Divide mushrooms among cups and crack 1 egg into each. Bake in middle of oven until whites are cooked but yolks are still runny, about 15 minutes. Remove (with ham) from muffin cups carefully, using 2 spoons or small spatulas. Season with salt and pepper.

Serves 12

Innkeeper Tidbit:
You may need to test several types of ham before you come up with the one you like. We look for round, Virginia prepackaged ham slices.

French Sorrel Quiche

Who said real men don't eat quiche? You wouldn't know it by the clean plates coming back to the kitchen after this breakfast at Tiffany Hill!

> **1 (9-inch) ready-made pie crust (thawed)**
> **½ cup fresh French sorrel, thinly sliced**
> **½ cup Swiss cheese, shredded**
> **1 egg**
> **½ cup milk**
> **Dash of nutmeg**

Preheat oven to 375°.

Cut pie crust and place to fit in two 6 oz. ramekins. Divide the French sorrel and cheese equally between the ramekins. In a medium bowl, whisk egg, milk, and nutmeg together. Pour egg mixture into ramekins. Put ramekins onto baking sheet and place in oven. Bake 35 to 40 minutes or until the cheese is golden brown.

Serves 2

Innkeeper Tidbit:
If French sorrel is not available, you can substitute fresh or frozen spinach. If using frozen, thaw first and squeeze very dry. This recipe has been a favorite in Kate's home for many years and is great to serve for family gatherings.

Greek Frittata

Thank you Clare, for adding a wonderful recipe to our collection! You might have to get up a bit early to get this one going, but I assure you, your guests will love you for it! I know my "camp friends" loved it when I tested it on them!

1½ cups Feta cheese	1 small can of artichoke hearts, rough cut
1½ cups Mozzarella cheese	1 cup red onion, diced
½ cup Parmesan cheese	2 Tbsp. red wine vinegar
1 tsp. oregano	1 tsp. black pepper
1 tsp. basil	8 eggs
1 pint grape tomatoes, halved	2 cups milk

Preheat oven to 275°.

Spray 9 by 13-inch baking dish with cooking spray. Layer all ingredients except eggs and milk in baking dish, reserving some of the Mozzarella and Parmesan cheeses for the top. Whisk eggs and milk together. Pour egg mixture over the top of arranged ingredients. Wrap tight with aluminum foil. Bake for 1½ hours at 275°. Remove foil and sprinkle with remaining Mozzarella and Parmesan cheese. Increase temperature to 325° and bake until brown.

Serves 10-12

Innkeeper Tidbit:
We arrange the frittata ingredients the night before and then add the egg mixture in the morning to reduce prep time.

Hash Brown Casserole with Chive Eggs

We searched high and low for a hash brown recipe to serve on Tiffany Hill. Then, I remembered that I had served one in the 80's! After digging through tons of recipes, I found it! Recently, a guest even wrote about this dish in the guest comment book. It's a keeper!

1 (20 oz.) bag Simply Potatoes
½ cup sour cream
1 can cream of celery soup
1 cup Cheddar cheese, grated
1 tsp. salt
1 stick of butter, melted
1 cup cornflakes, crushed

Chive Eggs
1 Tbsp. butter
20 eggs
Chopped chives

Preheat oven to 350°.

Combine potatoes, sour cream, celery soup, cheese, salt and ½ of the melted butter. Spoon the mixture into individual ramekins. Mix remaining butter and corn flakes. Sprinkle on top of mixture. Bake for 30 minutes or until golden brown.

Chive Eggs: We use 2 eggs per person and scramble them exactly how Cass showed me. It's easy! Spray skillet with cooking spray. Melt 1 Tbsp. butter over low heat. Crack each egg into skillet. DO NOT add any water or milk. As eggs cook, softly fold over with spatula. Top with chives and serve.

Serves 10

Innkeeper Tidbit:
All ingredients, except the topping, can be mixed the night before and then just scooped into individual ramekins the next morning. Add the topping, and in the oven they go!

Lemon Basil Soufflé

I have always admired cooks who could master a soufflé, so I was thrilled when our very own Breakfast Chef, Kate, developed this soufflé for our guests!

½ **Tbsp. water**
¼ **tsp. baking powder**
1 egg
½ **tsp. sour cream**
3 drops hot sauce
Dash of fresh basil
½ **tsp. lemon zest**
¼ **cup Gouda cheese**, grated

Preheat oven to 350°. Grease individual soufflé ramekin.

First, combine water and baking powder. Then, add egg and sour cream and beat until fully incorporated. Next, add hot sauce, basil, and lemon zest. Mix well. Stir in cheese. Pour into prepared dish and bake for 15 minutes. Serve immediately.

Serves 1

Innkeeper Tidbit:
The first time we served this to guests, we asked for their feedback. We will never forget Evan's instant reaction; "Surprisingly refreshing!" Now that's some good feedback!

Sunrise Pot Pie by D'vine Kitchen

Love this creation by D'vine Kitchen! Of course, I love Southern pot pies and am thrilled to have a breakfast version. Thanks, Donna, for coming up with this one!

1 cup cooked pork sausage, crumbled
1 Idaho potato, peeled and diced
1 cup prepared white gravy
3 scrambled eggs (see note below)
Salt and pepper
1 sheet thawed puff pastry
Egg wash (1 beaten egg with 1 Tbsp. water)

Preheat oven to 350°.

Spray 6 ramekins with cooking spray. Warm sausage in skillet over medium heat and set aside. Sauté potatoes in the same skillet as the sausage for 10 to 12 minutes, or until potatoes are tender and slightly golden. Mix together sausage, potatoes and gravy. Divide into ramekins. In a separate heated skillet, scramble eggs until set but still very moist. Salt and pepper the eggs to taste. Layer the eggs on top of sausage mixture in ramekins.

Roll out puff pastry and cut into 6 squares larger than diameter of ramekin. Place pastry on top of ramekins and brush with egg wash. Place on cookie sheet and bake for 30 minutes or until golden brown.

Serves 6

Innkeeper Tidbit:
When preparing scrambled eggs for this recipe, only cook the eggs till set, but not dry. Eggs will continue to cook inside the pot pie, and will be perfect when the dish comes out of the oven!

Three Cheese Egg Croissants

This is another guest favorite, graciously given to me by Rachel, cook extraordinaire. We changed up our cheese mixture to make it our own. So easy to prep the night before and slip into the oven in the morning. Your guests will think you worked all morning!

**10 croissants, cut into top and
  bottom halves
½ cup white Cheddar cheese,
  grated
½ cup smoked Gouda cheese,
  grated
Brie cheese dollops**

**10 eggs
1½ cups milk
¾ tsp. cayenne pepper
1/8 tsp. salt**

Lightly grease 10 ramekins with cooking spray. Slice croissants in half lengthwise and place the bottoms in the ramekins. Sprinkle each croissant bottom with the 3 cheeses. In medium bowl, whisk the eggs, milk and seasonings together. Pour over croissants and cheeses. Place tops of croissants on ramekins.

Cover and place in refrigerator overnight.

In the morning, preheat oven to 350°.

Bake for 30 minutes or until eggs are set and the croissants are golden brown.

Serves 10

Innkeeper Tidbit:
You can also add ham for a variation to this recipe.

Ultimate Cheese Omelet with Southern Grits

Our limit on omelets is four unless guests have different seating times. Four burners = four omelets.

Per Omelet
2 eggs
2 tsp. water
1 tsp. butter
1 tsp. white cheddar cheese
1 tsp. Parmesan cheese
1 tsp. Swiss cheese
1 Tbsp. salsa (optional)

Southern Grits
1 cup Nora Mill Stone Ground Grits
2 cups water
1 cup half & half
½ stick butter
Salt to taste

Omelet: Whisk eggs with water until fluffy. Over medium heat, melt butter in an 8-inch skillet. Pour egg mixture in and allow it to start cooking. As the eggs start to set, lift edges to allow uncooked egg to pour into pan. When eggs are set, sprinkle with cheeses. Fold over in pan. Transfer to plate and top with salsa.

Southern Grits: Bring water and half & half to a boil. Slowly add in grits while stirring. Reduce heat. Add butter and salt and simmer until cooked, stirring occasionally.

Serves 1

Innkeeper Tidbit:
Linda Hayes, my long-time friend and B&B mentor helped me discover the secret of great omelets – water! Simply adding a bit of water to your eggs makes them light and fluffy.

Breakfast at Tiffany's

Candlelight makes breakfast extra special!

Dessert Course

Caramelized Banana Pudding by D'vine Kitchen

Carlee's One-Step Pound Cake

Chocolate Molten Cake

Cinnamon Bread Pudding

Fruit Crumble by D'vine Kitchen

Kate's Lemon Cream Pie

Peanut Butter Pie

Pear Crostata

Peppermint Brownie Trifle by D'vine Kitchen

Petite Banana Split Parfait

Raspberry Lemonade Pie

Signature Pineapple Pudding

Strawberry Crepes

Caramelized Banana Pudding by D'vine Kitchen

What a beautiful and easy dessert prepared by D'vine Kitchen. No need for a torch to caramelize the meringue. Simply use the oven, but keep an eye on it. When they turn golden brown, they are ready to come out.

½ cup brown sugar, firmly packed
¼ cup butter
¼ tsp. ground cinnamon
½ cup pecans, chopped
4 large ripe bananas, sliced

1 small package (3.4 oz.) of
   vanilla pudding mix
4 large egg whites
¼ cup granulated sugar
48 vanilla wafers

Preheat oven to 325°.

Cook first 4 ingredients in a large skillet over medium heat, stirring constantly, 2 to 3 minutes or until bubbly. Add bananas; cook another 2 to 3 minutes or until thoroughly heated. Remove from heat. Make pudding according to package directions.

Divide half of banana mixture, pudding, and wafers among 8 ramekins or ovenproof glass dishes. Layer with the remaining banana mixture, pudding, and wafers. Beat egg whites at high speed with an electric mixer until foamy. Add ¼ cup sugar, 1 Tbsp. at a time, beating until stiff peaks form and sugar dissolves (2 to 4 minutes). Spread meringue over ramekins. Place ramekins on a baking sheet. Bake for 15 to 20 minutes, or until the meringue is golden. Let cool on a wire rack for 30 minutes.

Serves 8

Courage is abundant in the abstract.

Innkeeper Tidbit:
This is a recipe that can be prepared the night before. We like to prep for breakfast beforehand so that we can sleep in too!

Carlee's One-Step Pound Cake

The easiest ever pound cake! Pair with Chocolate Butter Cream Frosting for an always requested family favorite!

2 ¼ cups all-purpose or unbleached flour
2 cups sugar
½ tsp. salt
½ tsp. baking soda

1 cup dairy sour cream
1 cup salted butter, softened
1 tsp. vanilla extract
3 eggs

Preheat oven to 325°.

Generously grease (using 1 Tbsp. solid shortening) and lightly flour 12 cup tube pan. In large bowl, blend all ingredients at low speed until moistened. Beat 3 minutes at medium speed. Pour batter into prepared pan. Bake for 60 minutes or until top is golden brown and cake pulls away from side of pan and toothpick comes out clean. When lukewarm; invert onto plate and cool completely. Remove from pan, then wrap in foil and freeze. When ready to use, cut in layers and frost with Chocolate Butter Cream Frosting.

Chocolate Butter Cream Frosting

2 cups semi-sweet chocolate pieces
½ cup boiling water
8 egg yolks
1 tsp. vanilla extract
2 sticks butter, softened

Empty the chocolate bits into a blender. Add boiling water, cover, and blend on high speed for 20 seconds. Turn off blender. Add egg yolks and vanilla. Cover and blend on high speed. Remove top and add butter sticks, one at a time, until well blended. Refrigerate until frosting is a spreading consistency. Microwave frosting for 30 second intervals, stirring in between if too stiff for spreading.

Serves 16 to 20

Innkeeper Tidbit:
Self-rising flour is not recommended for the cake. To change up the glaze, omit vanilla and substitute bourbon or brandy in place of the water to add extra flavor!

Chocolate Molten Cake

A fabulous dessert and SO easy to make! You will wow your guests with your culinary skills on this one!

1 cup unsalted butter, softened	**4 large egg yolks**
8 oz. semi-sweet chocolate	**½ cup sugar**
4 large eggs	**4 tsp. all-purpose flour**
	Ice cream

Preheat oven to 450°.

Heat butter and chocolate in microwave at half power, until chocolate is melted. When melted, stir together and set aside. Meanwhile, in the bowl of an electric mixer, whisk eggs, egg yolks, and sugar until light and thick. Slowly add chocolate mixture to mixer. Add flour, and mix until combined. Divide the batter equally between 8 ramekins. Place on a baking sheet and transfer to oven. Bake for 10 to 13 minutes. Sides should be set and centers soft. Top with a scoop of ice cream and serve.

Serves 8

Make time to make memories.

Innkeeper Tidbit:
When we first started to make these, we would remove them from the ramekins. Sometimes, they came out perfect, but one time the chocolate just ran all over the plate. Since then, they are served in the same ramekins they bake in! Absolutely delicious either way!

Cinnamon Bread Pudding

My all-time favorite dessert is bread pudding. This one is a real crowd pleaser with the cinnamon raisin bread and the Whiskey White Chocolate Sauce! Enjoy!

3 Tbsp. butter, melted
¾ cup sugar
2 cups milk
3 large eggs
2 tsp. vanilla extract
1 loaf cinnamon raisin bread, torn into 1 inch pieces

Whiskey White Chocolate Sauce
1 cup whipping cream
4 (1 oz.) white chocolate baking squares, chopped
½ oz. whiskey
Ice cream

Preheat oven to 350°.

Spray 10 ramekins with cooking spray. Drizzle butter into ramekins. Whisk sugar, milk, eggs and vanilla together. Stir in bread. Spoon into ramekins. Bake 25 to 30 minutes.

For the sauce, cook whipping cream in saucepan over medium heat, stirring often. Whisk in white chocolate and whiskey until chocolate is melted. Spoon over bread pudding, top with ice cream, and serve.

Serves 10

Attention to detail is important!

Innkeeper Tidbit:
Bread Pudding can be prepped the night before and popped in the oven the next morning to bake.

Fruit Crumble by D'vine Kitchen

Donna from D'vine Kitchen never ceases to amaze me with how she can simply whip something together. I had overstocked the pantry with granola and we were discussing how it could be used. Before I knew it, she had whipped up this fruit crumble. Simply delicious!

Fruit of choice, approximately 2 cups
6 tsp. flour
½ tsp. nutmeg

2 cups granola
2 Tbsp. brown sugar
2 Tbsp. butter, softened
Ice cream

Preheat oven to 350°.

Stir in one teaspoon of flour per portion of fruit and sprinkle with nutmeg. Spray ramekins with cooking spray and fill with fruit mixture. Add a few teaspoons of water or apple juice if fruit seems dry. Mix granola, brown sugar and butter together. Layer the granola mixture over the fruit mixture, to cover. Bake for 20 minutes. Top with a scoop of ice cream and serve.

Serves 6

"Food is Love."
Donna Southwick,
D'vine Kitchen

Innkeeper Tidbit:
Recipe can be made with peaches, apples, pears, pineapple, blueberries, or raspberries. If using apples, add 2 Tbsp. apple juice and dried cranberries.

Kate's Lemon Cream Pie

What a great addition to Tiffany Hill's dessert repertoire! Just like Kate, who became our first Breakfast Chef on Tiffany Hill!

4 tsp. grated lemon zest
4 large egg yolks
1 (14 oz.) can sweetened
condensed milk

½ cup strained juice from 3 or 4
lemons
8 mini graham cracker crusts
Whipped cream (garnish)
Lemon twist (garnish)

Preheat oven to 325°.

To make the filling, whisk together lemon zest and egg yolks in medium bowl until fully incorporated, about 2 minutes. Beat in sweetened condensed milk, then lemon juice; set aside at room temperature to thicken. Prepare the crust while the mixture sets. Allow approximately 20 minutes.

To prepare crusts, bake until lightly browned and fragrant, about 5 minutes.

Pour lemon filling into warm crusts; bake until centers are set but still slightly soft, 15 to 17 minutes. Cool pies to room temperature. Refrigerate until well chilled, at least 3 hours. Garnish with whipped cream and a lemon twist.

Serves 8

We become what we speak.

Innkeeper Tidbit:
You can substitute Key Lime for the lemon and create an amazing Key Lime pie as well.

Peanut Butter Pie

This one is from Rachel. It is easy to prepare ahead of time and freeze, so that it's ready whenever you need it. What a great tutor you were in preparing breakfast for Tiffany Hill's guests. They will forever more enjoy the wonderful recipes you shared with me!

4 oz. cream cheese, softened
1 cup confectioners' sugar
½ cup creamy peanut butter
½ cup milk
8 oz. container non-dairy
whipped topping

1 graham cracker crust,
baked and cooled
¼ cup salted peanuts,
finely chopped
Shaved chocolate

Whip cream cheese until fluffy. Beat in sugar and peanut butter. Slowly add milk, blending thoroughly into mixture. Fold whipped topping into mixture. Pour into baked pie shell. Sprinkle with chopped peanuts. You may also want to surround the pie with shaved chocolate pieces, as shown in the photo. Freeze until firm. Wrap in freezer paper after pie is frozen for storage.

Serves 12

Don't look back ....
no longer an option!

Innkeeper Tidbit:
Drizzle with chocolate sauce
and they will lick their plates!

Pear Crostata

This is amazingly simple, yet elegant in its presentation. A fabulous dessert for the Fall. Top with a dollop of vanilla ice cream and be prepared to wow your guests!

15 oz. can pears (in own juice, drained)
2 Tbsp. brown sugar
1 rolled pie crust
1 small can almond pie filling
4 Tbsp. slivered almonds

Preheat oven to 350°.

Mix pears and brown sugar together. Set aside. Cut pie crust into four 5 inch rounds. Spread approximately 2 Tbsp. of almond filling in center of the pie crust leaving about an inch around the edges. Divide pear mixture evenly and place on top of the almond filling. Sprinkle with slivered almonds. Fold edges of the crust to the center of the filling, leaving the center open to create a pinwheel. Place on baking sheet and bake for 15 to 20 minutes or until golden brown and filling is bubbling.

Serves 4

You have to experience the sadness of leaving, before you can experience the joy of returning!

Innkeeper Tidbit:
Add cranberries and nutmeg to give this dessert additional Fall flavor. Apples or peaches can also be used for variations.

Peppermint Brownie Trifle by D'vine Kitchen

What a fun dessert, especially for St. Patrick's Day celebrations! Easy to do with brownies made ahead of time.

Chocolate sauce
4 baked brownies
6 York Peppermint Patties
Whipped topping

Drizzle chocolate sauce in the bottom of trifle glasses. Cut brownies into ½-inch squares. Chop 4 peppermint patties into pieces. Cut two peppermint patties into wedges for garnish. Layer brownie pieces, peppermint pattie pieces, and whipped topping in glasses twice. Garnish with peppermint pattie wedge.

Serves 10

Happiness is having something to look forward to.

Innkeeper Tidbit:
Feel free to "kick it up a notch". Drizzle with Crème de Menthe or top with green sugar sprinkles!

Petite Banana Split Parfait

One weekend after we opened the test kitchen, we whipped up this easy dessert and it was an instant favorite. Thanks to the guests on Tiffany Hill, the dessert has a name.

10 Lady Fingers
1 small can crushed pineapple
½ cup prepared vanilla pudding
2 bananas

Chocolate syrup
Whipped cream
3 strawberries, cut in chunks

In each petite martini glass, break one lady finger into 3 pieces. Add 1 tsp. crushed pineapple with juice. Top with dollop of pudding. Insert three banana slices around the side of dish.   Drizzle 1 Tbsp. chocolate syrup over pudding.   Top with whipped cream and strawberries.

Serves 10

You never get a second chance to make a first impression.

Innkeeper Tidbit:
We use vanilla pudding in our parfaits, but you could turn it into a classic petite banana split with a scoop of ice cream.

Raspberry Lemonade Pie

Another one of Rachel's secret weapons and guests love it! Thank you, Rachel, for sharing this Southern Living recipe with me!

> **1 (14 oz.) can sweetened condensed milk**
> **1 (6 oz.) can frozen lemonade**
> **3 Tbsp. seedless raspberry preserves**
> **1 (8 oz.) container frozen whipped topping**
> **1 graham cracker crust,**
>   **baked and cooled**

Whisk first 3 ingredients together in a large bowl until smooth. Fold whipped topping into mixture. Pour into baked pie shell. Freeze until firm. Cut into slices, then top with whipped cream and a fresh raspberry.

Serves 12

You can do all things through Him who strengthens you.

Innkeeper Tidbit:
I use the 12 piece graham cracker crust found in the baking section of your grocery.

Signature Pineapple Pudding

Tiffany Hill would not be the same without this wonderful pudding. I first tasted it one Easter at the home of Laura and Dean Crawley, as prepared each year by Dorothy Meyers, for special dinners. I just knew I wanted to make this dish for my guests on Tiffany Hill. I gave my word that I would keep it "in the family". But now, with Dorothy's permission, everyone can enjoy this wonderful pudding!

1 stick butter
3 eggs
1 cup sugar
½ cup milk

Dash of salt
1 (20 oz.) can pineapple chunks,
 drained
8 slices of white bread (crust
 removed and cubed)

Preheat oven to 350°.

Melt butter and let cool. In a mixing bowl, beat eggs well. Next, add sugar, milk and salt, and then add the pineapple and melted butter. Add cubed bread and mix until well coated. Pour mixture into a 1 ½ quart casserole dish and bake for 30 minutes.

Serves 6

"I'm living proof that
Dreams Do Come True!"
~ Selena

Innkeeper Tidbit:
I will never forget a special guest who was on the Hill with her three daughters. Each morning she said, "No dessert for me today". But when it came to the Pineapple Pudding, not only did she ask for a serving, she asked for seconds!

Strawberry Crepes

We always see clean plates returned to the kitchen with this creamy, light dessert. This dessert pairs perfectly with a hearty, savory breakfast.

6 pre-made crepes
8 oz. strawberry cream cheese
3 fresh strawberries, diced
10 oz. jar strawberry jam or preserves
¼ cup water

6 fresh strawberries cut into
 spears, for garnish
Whipped cream, for garnish

Spread approximately two tablespoons of strawberry cream cheese lengthwise in center of each crepe. Sprinkle diced strawberries evenly into crepes. Loosely roll each crepe. In a medium saucepan, mix strawberry jam and water. Cook over medium heat, stirring constantly until mixture begins to boil then remove from heat. Serve warm syrup over crepes. Garnish with whipped cream and strawberry spear.

Serves 6

People ask me, "Aren't you proud of what you have done?" My answer... "I am humbled by what I've been given to do!"

Innkeeper Tidbit:
If you open the refrigerator and find you are out of strawberry cream cheese, simply whip together fresh diced strawberries with 8 oz. of regular cream cheese.

Before There Was Breakfast... There Was A Dream

For more than 25 years, I dreamt of owning a bed and breakfast. I could picture myself in a huge house welcoming guests, cooking delicious breakfasts, and plumping pillows for the sweet dreams of weary travelers. But while I had a career in corporate America, I hadn't been born with a silver spoon in my mouth; how could I possibly take on such an endeavor? Yet no matter how many times I turned away, the dream remained. A dear friend once told me that if something has been placed in your heart for so long and you just can't seem to shake it, well, it might just be from God. Building a B&B was a dream that I could not shake. I just had to figure out how to make it happen.

Do You Have A Dream?

What are the deepest desires you cradle in your heart? Where do your passions lie? Dreams come in all shapes and sizes, so I'm not just talking to future innkeepers. Perhaps your desire is to travel Europe, to become a master gardener, to lose 100 pounds, to achieve an early retirement, or to turn your hobby into a business. No matter where you are starting from, or where you wish to go, I am here to tell you that courage is abundant in the abstract — you need only take the first step.

Where Do You Begin?

There is a precious passage in Psalms declaring that God's word is a lamp unto our feet. I've spent a great deal of time meditating on this promise. Often, our fears are rooted in the unknown. For some, uncertainty is exciting. But for many, the immense mystery of where our dreams might lead us is enough to deter us from even beginning the journey.

But take a moment to envision yourself standing at the helm of a dark road, gripping the handle of a lantern. Although you cannot see what's around you, your path is clear, visible under a certain light. With each new step forward, the lamp leads to a new illuminated area. Like this lamp-lit path, don't expect to know precisely what direction your dream will take you — you'll risk disappointment if the road veers even slightly off course — rather, focus on the end result, embrace the uncertainty, and release some control. With your dream as the lamp that lights your feet, I promise you will find great joy in the journey.

First Steps

After having this starry-eyed dream for so many years, there came a point where I knew I needed to do something. I needed to stop just thinking about it and take real action. Even if I made mistakes, even if I was wrong, I knew that I wouldn't feel fulfilled unless I did *something*.

Step 1 ~ Let Others Know About Your Dream

In 1999, I sent a letter to all of my friends, declaring with certainty that I would open a bed and breakfast in five years. In doing so, I created a network of accountability partners. This should be your first step. Let others in on your goals and share with them your fears. Find accountability partners who will listen with love, but also challenge you to succeed. This could be friends, family, local business owners, or clergy members. The important thing is that you get the idea out there and be open to the feedback of others.

This first step is the hardest. Voicing your deepest desires leaves you a bit vulnerable. But I think you'll find yourself pleasantly surprised by how much support rolls in from those who care about you and your success. So many people want to encourage someone with a dream.

Step 2 ~ Put Your Thoughts On Paper

In an exercise often referred to as mind mapping, take a piece of blank paper and write down every single thing you can think of that would have to happen to make your dream come true. Think BIG, think small, think logistics, think time, think people. Let your mind wander and put it all on paper.

Be specific. Do you need a business plan? Do you need a marketing plan? Do you need a financial plan? Do you need a floor plan? Ask yourself what you need and it will start to open the doors. My list had a *lot* of items but I wasn't going to know where to start until I had that list.

Step 3 ~ Start Doing

Once I had my list, I could start checking items off. I started a side business, went to inn-keeping seminars, created an investment club for women, started inn-sitting for established B&B's, and even launched a marketing campaign called *Dreambuilders* where I began taking reservation deposits for room nights. (I was amazed, to say the least, when I amassed two months of reservations for an inn that didn't even exist!)

Step 4 ~ Push Through Disappointment

In 2004, I had yet to achieve my dream. I had taken a lot of steps but I was disappointed that I hadn't met my five-year goal. I found myself talking the talk without walking the walk. Determined to push through my disappointment, I reached out to experts who could help me transition from dream to reality. I used a team of professionals — from financial consultants to real estate agents to marketing specialists — to advise me along my path. With their help I armed myself with a business plan, a logo, a floor plan, and a recommitment to my mission. I picked up that figurative lamp to my feet and started walking again.

Your Actions Become Achievement

In 2007, I was part of a corporate downsizing and had to make a choice. Do I continue in corporate America or do I make the leap of faith and follow my dream full-time? Because of the steps I'd already taken and with a lot of additional hard work and perseverance, I made the decision that it was time to take that leap. With my faith behind me, the pieces started falling into place and I saw my life's dream fulfilled in June of 2009. It took everything I have to get to this point and there are still days that it takes all of me to keep it going, but I've never been happier. As the plaque in my library says, "You are never given a dream without also being given the power to make it come true." (Richard Bach) I am living proof that dreams do come true!

It's Your Turn. What's The Worst That Can Happen?

There was a pivotal point in my journey when someone asked me, "What is the worst thing that can happen if you pursue your dream?" Think about that question and what your answer would be. For me, the worst thing that could have happened was to grow old and look back on my life knowing that I hadn't tried. The thought of that potential disappointment in myself propelled me — energized me — to continue moving forward along the path.

Today, after years of one foot in front of the other, letting the lamp light my path, I've reached a point where I'm having the time of my life. I was fortunate to try, I was blessed to succeed, and I know without a doubt that I have done what I was put on this Earth to do. That gives me a peace that surpasses all understanding.

This book is another chapter in a dream fulfilled. From the delicious recipes to the stunning imagery and engaging anecdotes, these pages were pored over with prayers for you, my dear reader. It is my hope that you've become both excited and inspired by what you've seen, and that you too will take that first step in faith toward your dream.

Psalm 119:105

Selena Einwechter
Dreamer/Owner/Innkeeper